LIVING AND SHARING YOUR FAITH

Grace Pathway Milestone 4.1

BILL GIOVANNETTI

© Copyright 2020 Bill Giovannetti. All Rights Reserved.

No part of this book may be reproduced or transmitted in any form or by any means, digital, electronic or mechanical, including photocopying, recording, or by an information storage and retrieval system—except by a reviewer who may quote brief passages in a review to be printed in a magazine, newspaper, or on the Web—without permission in writing from the publisher.

Although the author and publisher have made every effort to ensure the accuracy and completeness of information contained in this book, the same assumes no responsibility for errors, inaccuracies, omissions, or any inconsistency herein. Any slights of people, places, or organizations are unintentional. All persons and situations mentioned in this book are fictionalized. Any resemblance to any person, living or dead, is strictly coincidental. Nothing herein shall be construed as a substitute for personal, pastoral, or professional counseling or therapy.

ISBN E-book edition: 978-1-946654-20-5

ISBN Print edition: 978-1-946654-21-2

All scripture quotations, unless otherwise indicated, are taken from the *New King James Version* (R). Copyright © 1982 by Thomas Nelson, Inc. Used by permission. All rights reserved.

Scripture quotations marked (NLT) are taken from the *Holy Bible, New Living Translation,* copyright © 1996, 2004, 2007 by Tyndale House Foundation. Used by permission of Tyndale House Publishers, Inc., Carol Stream, Illinois 60188. All rights reserved.

Scriptures marked NAS95 taken from the NEW AMERICAN STANDARD BIBLE, Copyright © 1960, 1962, 1963 1968, 1971, 1972, 1973 1975, 1977, 1995 by The Lockman Foundation. All rights reserved. Used by permission. http://www.Lockman.org

For additional resources, please visit maxgrace.com.

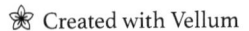

❀ Created with Vellum

CONTENTS

Part One
LIVING YOUR FAITH

1. The Story of Your Life — 3
2. The Nature of Sanctification — 9
3. The Power of Sanctification — 16
4. The Process of Sanctification — 22
5. The Struggle of Sanctification — 32
6. The Results of Sanctification — 37
7. The Fruit of Sanctification — 42

Part Two
SHARING YOUR FAITH

8. The Nature of Evangelism — 53
9. Pre-Evangelism — 57
10. Three Principles of Evangelism — 63
11. The Gospel Message — 68
12. Tying the Knot — 73
13. Then What? — 81
   What's Next? — 83

LIVING YOUR FAITH

THE STORY OF YOUR LIFE

Your life is sending a message. Every single day, you are telling the story of what you believe about yourself, your life, your God, and your world.

In God's great design, the message you will send is one of grace, love, truth, and joy. The world needs that desperately, don't you think?

As a child of God, you are designed to show forth "Christ in you." You are a living, breathing monument to the matchless grace of God. St Paul said to his friends, "You are our epistle written in our hearts, known and read by all men" (2 Corinthians 3:2).

"Out of one hundred people, one will read the Bible and the other ninety-nine will read the Christian." So said a great, old-time preacher named D.L. Moody.

Another preacher of yesteryear, Gypsy Smith, said, "There are five Gospels—Matthew, Mark, Luke, John, and the Christian—but most people never read the first four."

Your life can have a powerful testimony in the world. As we move deeper into the Grace Pathway, the goal is that our family, friends, teammates, classmates, neighbors, and even our enemies see a three-dimensional example of the power and grace of God.

In this book, I'd like to invite you to so fill your heart with God's love, that the story of your life is a testament of grace. Let's dig deep into the topic of living and sharing your faith.

THE STRUGGLE

Anyone who has been a Christian for a while knows this is harder than it seems.

Sometimes, it feels as if our hearts are telling two stories—two completely opposite, contradictory stories. One of life and grace, but another of dysfunction and shame. One of kindness and peace, but another of selfishness and drama.

There are deeply embedded lies that make it hard to live and share your faith.

Those lies have a nasty habit of popping up when you least want them to.

You can't help it. Your deepest beliefs have a way of coming out in words, thoughts, and actions. Your thoughts, your instincts, and your knee-jerk reactions, bubble up from the most deeply embedded convictions in your soul.

God has a name for the process of changing those most deeply embedded convictions: *repentance*. Repentance does not mean some kind of dramatic, tearful announcement of your intention to be a better person. No. Repentance is you submitting your mind and heart to the Word of God so that, by the Spirit of God, you can "be renewed in the spirit of your mind" (Ephesians 4:23).

This is how God changes a life.

This takes time.

This is also extremely important because your life is meant to be a living, breathing exhibition of the grace and truth of God in the midst of a messed up, crazy, and painful world.

> Do all things without complaining and disputing, that you may become blameless and harmless, children of God without fault in the midst of a crooked and perverse generation, among whom you shine as lights in the world. (Philippians 2:14, 15)

This is you at your best. This is the person God designed you to be. When you dig through all the layers of your heart, and peer into your deepest longings, you will find an unshakeable desire to walk with God.

A desire to "shine as a light" for Jesus.

That desire is there. It may be a bit buried. But it is there. It is part of the real you.

THE TRUEST DESIRE

God Himself put that desire there. He implanted it deep inside you. It will never go away. If you are a Christian, you are a "new creation" (2 Corinthians 5:17). Your salvation gave you a new nature. There is a new life, a new essence, a new power pulsing in your heart. This new life longs to follow the steps of Jesus.

We will talk about the exact source of this new life and its longings more later.

Sometimes, however, this holy desire gets buried by an avalanche of troubles, pains, temptations, and distractions. Sometimes you feel weak. Sometimes you feel conflicting desires.

Welcome to the real world.

This struggle is real. It is both normal and abnormal. It is *normal* because we all feel it. The greatest missionary-teacher of early Christianity confessed: "For the good that I will to do, I do not do; but the evil I will not to do, that I practice" (Romans 7:19). If Paul felt that internal conflict, it's normal that we all do.

But the conflict is *abnormal* too. It's abnormal because when you live according to your new nature, you will do what comes naturally. But, when you live against your new nature, you're doing something unnatural.

For an unsaved person, who has not been given a new nature, acting against the will of God is the most natural thing in the world. They are acting in line with their fallen nature.

But, for a saved person, who has a new nature—redeemed, and holy, and powerful, and good—every sin is an act *against* your nature. You are living crossways to the life that has been implanted in you. This is abnormal. It creates a spiritual dissonance within you that plays out in your emotions, relationships, and psychology. It is not God's plan for you.

I'm glad God's grace never goes away.

The good news is that the life of Christ can, and will, shine through you. This is not really about you making something happen. It is more about you "letting" something happen:

- Let the peace of God rule in your heart (Colossians 3:15).
- Let the Word of Christ dwell in you richly (Colossians 3:16).
- Let your gentleness be known to all (Philippians 4:5).

- Let your speech be seasoned with grace (Colossians 4:6).
- Let your conduct be worthy of the gospel (Philippians 1:27).
- Let your light shine before the world (Matthew 5:16).

The idea is that all these things are natural, and native, and normal for the child of God. They happen, not by our power, but by His.

When the machinery of grace in our lives is running smoothly, these—and many other wonderful qualities—will be the end product.

We will bring forth fruit, and the funny thing is, it won't feel like effort or sacrifice, it will feel like just being our truest, deepest selves.

The church will benefit by your presence as a mature child of God.

The world will benefit by your presence as a witness to the saving work of Christ.

LIVING AND SHARING

In the first part of this book, you will learn about *living* your faith. This is the process the Bible calls *sanctification*. It is how God makes you more and more like Jesus.

In the second part of this book, you will learn about *sharing* your faith. This is called *evangelism*, and we will talk about how we can be intentional about it without being offensive.

God *saves* you. God *blesses* you. God *grows* you. Amen.

The outcome of the first three milestones on the Grace Pathway is this: God *uses* you. You matter in this world. Even if you're not famous, or up front, or impressive. You make a difference. The Bible compares you to a vessel, used for storage. What is God storing in you? The glorious treasures of His grace (2 Corinthians 4:7). Now, it's time to let those treasures overflow to a lost and needy world.

Your life is sending a message, one way or another.

Let's make sure that our message sings the mighty power and saving grace of our best friend and only Savior, the Lord Jesus Christ.

THE NATURE OF SANCTIFICATION

One of the most important questions for Christians to ask is simple, but often overlooked. It is the question, *How does God change a person's life?*

We might have some idea of how a school changes a person's life. Or of how family changes a person's life. We have probably seen how church, or friendships, or temptations can change a person's life.

But how exactly does God change a person's life?

That question is what sanctification is all about.

Let's draw on some of the theology we have already learned. Hopefully you recall justification when you learned about The Cross (Milestone 3.2).

Justification means that God declares you righteous, based upon the imputed righteousness of Christ.

Remember?

Hopefully you'll also remember when a person is justified. Justification happens at the very moment a person is saved. It is instantaneous. It is eternal. It is once for all and it is finished.

But justification alone is not final—there's more to the story.

Your justification triggered a launch sequence in your life. Because, in the nano-second you were justified, God in heaven pressed a button and launched sanctification into your life too.

WHAT IS SANCTIFICATION?

The word 'sanctification' is part of a family of words. The cousins include: sanctify, holy, holiness, and saint. The second-cousins include: edification, edify, consecration, dedication, yielding, and surrender.

The root word of sanctify is the Latin word *sanctus*, which means holy.

Holy means whole, wholesome, innocent, and morally pure. It means set apart from evil and set apart to God. To be holy is to live up to God's expectations. To be unholy is to fall short of God's expectations.

His expectations are high indeed: "Be holy, for I am holy" (1 Peter 1:16 quoting Leviticus 11:45).

To be sanctified means to be made holy.

Sanctification, then, is the way God sees a person as holy in His sight, and then makes that person holy in the real world. In your relationships, your family, your workplace, your school, your team, your everywhere.

How does God Himself change a person's life? Through sanctification.

No duties, transformations, behaviors, improvement, righteousness, obligations, "oughts," "shoulds," surrender, obedience, yielding, or good works in a Christian's life can happen outside the sphere of sanctification.

Louis Berkhof, a theologian of the early 1900s, defined sanctification this way:

> Sanctification may be defined as that gracious and continuous operation of the Holy Spirit, by which He delivers the justified sinner from the pollution of sin, renews his whole nature in the image of God, and enables him to perform good works.[1]

According to this definition, the power of sanctification is God the Holy Spirit. We are not sanctified by our power, but by His.

The process of sanctification involves deliverance from the pollution of sin—like wiping the mud off ourselves before entering the house.

Then it involves a renewal of our heart, character, words, thoughts, and deeds—like dressing up before sitting down for dinner.

In the process, God renews your whole nature. You are transformed from the inside out. It's as if you were a mirror, intended to reflect the goodness and love, the righteousness and power of God Himself. But the mirror is dirty, so, the reflection is distorted. In sanctification, God cleans the mud off of the mirror, then He polishes it to a high gloss.

The result is breathtaking.

When someone looks at you, they see you—the real, deepest, most beautiful you. But at the same time, they also see a reflection of the splendor of our majestic God.

> But we all, with unveiled face, beholding as in a mirror the glory of the Lord, are being transformed into the same image from glory to

glory, just as by the Spirit of the Lord. (2 Corinthians 3:18)

Like I said, breathtaking.

The indescribable beauty of God Himself reflected in your everyday life. That is the goal. That is the ever-receding finish line of God's work of sanctification in your life.

For our purposes, we'll use this simple definition:

> Sanctification is the grace-filled work of God in unburying you from the avalanche of sin, and enabling you to live every day with the holiness, joy, and love of Christ flowing through you.[2]

SANCTIFICATION AND JUSTIFICATION

One of the big mistakes Christians make is to jumble together justification and sanctification. This makes a theological mess.

It also makes a personal and emotional mess.

Because if you try to super-impose "living saved" (sanctification) on top of "getting saved" (justification), you create demands for behavior and performance that an unsaved person just can't achieve. The Christian message is transmogrified from the good news of a glorious gift into a disheartening list of chores.

Jumbling together justification and sanctification always results in legalism—imposing the lifestyle requirements of sanctification on top of the faith requirement of justification.

Get that?

Let's think of it this way.

Justification and Sanctification are twins, but they're not

identical twins. They are twins, in that, they are both born at the same time—the moment of your salvation.

But they are not identical twins, in that, they operate in different spheres and at different times. They must never be confused.

> — JUSTIFICATION AND SANCTIFICATION ARE TWINS, BUT THEY'RE NOT IDENTICAL TWINS.

Justification is the doorway to a *life*. Life with God. Life in God. Life from God. A new identity, nature, and being given freely to you with love from God.

Sanctification is the doorway to a *lifestyle*. This lifestyle expresses the adventure of living in a fallen world with Christ in your heart and holiness in your words, thoughts, and deeds.

Justification is a once-for-all event at the instant you were saved.

Sanctification is a lifelong process from the moment you were saved till you see Jesus face to face.

In justification, Jesus lived, died, and lives again for you.

In sanctification, you come alive, live, die, and live again for the Lord (Romans 14:8).

Justification is about getting saved.

Sanctification is about living saved.

In justification, God declares you righteous.

In sanctification, He makes you righteous.

They belong together, but they are different. Do not jumble them together.

Do not split them apart either. Justification is the on-switch to sanctification. The power of sanctification is switched on in your life the moment you receive Jesus.

There's no turning it off. When Jesus comes into your life, He doesn't come with an off-switch.

That means, for the rest of your life, He will be in you and with you. He will exert an inward tug toward the life you should and can be living.

Like it or not.

Even when you are stepping, or clicking, your way into a place you know you should not be, "Christ in you" will be pulling you the other way. He will be activating your conscience. He will be unmasking the dangers ahead. He will be turning dangerously sweet waters bitter, whenever the sweet lures you to evil. He will faithfully disturb your chosen path to sin and self-destruction. Jesus will never punish you for your sins, because your sins were paid in full at the Cross. Justice has been satisfied, once for all, and there can be no double jeopardy. You can erase divine punishment from your list of fears if you have been saved.

God will, however, "unshield" you from some of the consequences of your sinful choices—in this life—so that you will be "chastened by the Lord" (1 Corinthians 11:32).

Yes, He loves you that much.

You can't shut Him up, turn Him off, or shut Him down. Sanctification's engines never shut down.

You can, however, resist God. You can let temptation win the high ground. You can push back against God's sanctifying work. Again and again and again.

But if you were happy with that scenario, you wouldn't be reading this book. So let's assume better things.

Let's assume you want to go with the flow of God's sanctifying grace instead of against it.

This will become your daily, and even moment-by-moment, choice. In this book, we will learn how to put muscle behind this choice.

The most important thing to remember about sanctification is this: sanctification is God's work—beginning, middle, and end.

> — SANCTIFICATION IS GOD'S WORK—
> BEGINNING, MIDDLE, AND END.

God says, "I am the Lord, who sanctifies you" (Exodus 31:13, Leviticus 20:8, 22:32).

Paul writes, "For it is God who works in you both to will and to do for His good pleasure" (Philippians 2:13). Exactly who is performing the "works" in that verse?

Remember the big question: How does God change a person's life?

The operative word here is *God*.

Let's see what the Bible says about how God Himself makes you the person you've always longed to be.

---

1. Louis Berkhof, *Systematic Theology* (Grand Rapids: Wm. B. Eerdmans Publishing Co., 1938) p. 532.
2. Taken from *Know What You Believe (The Basics),* Milestone 3.3 in the Grace Pathway Series.

THE POWER OF SANCTIFICATION

The power of sanctification is God Himself. Anything less won't make the cut, and won't accomplish God's purposes. When we lean on our own human strength, we may impress other Christians, but we don't please God.

- "With him is an arm of flesh; but with us is the LORD our God, to help us and to fight our battles." (2 Chronicles 32:8)
- Thus says the LORD: "Cursed is the man who trusts in man / And makes flesh his strength, / Whose heart departs from the LORD." (Jeremiah 17:5)
- So he answered and said to me: "This is the word of the LORD to Zerubbabel: 'Not by might nor by power, but by My Spirit,' Says the LORD of hosts. (Zechariah 4:6)

All the good stuff of sanctification—good works, holiness, victory over sin, Christlike character, self-sacrifice, and love itself—requires the supernatural power and presence of God.

It is easy to forget this. It is easy to fuel our lives with human power, the "arm of flesh." When we forget the power of God, we produce a life that may look very good to our Christian friends, but does not please God.

In fact, God calls what we produce in this condition "dead works" (Hebrews 6:1; 9:14). He evaluates these dead works as worthless, and calls them "wood, hay, and straw," since they have no value in eternity (1 Corinthians 3:12-15).

Scripture describes some Christians as "carnal," which means fueled by human, fleshly power, instead of by the power of God (1 Corinthians 3:1-4).

God loves carnal Christians, and they will be in heaven someday.

Even though you might fall into a messed up, carnal condition, you still can't lose your salvation.[1]

That's grace!

In this state, a Christian might do some pretty nasty sins. Surprisingly, these same carnal Christians might also perform some good deeds that impress everyone — everyone, that is, except God.

That's because God is always looking at the heart (2 Corinthians 10:1-7). When His power and His presence flow in us, then, and only then, do our lifestyles please God and reflect His sanctifying power.

So how does that happen? How do we actually live day by day in the sanctifying power of God?

PLUGGING IN

Reasonable Christians will answer that question in different ways. There are differing theological views on sanctification.

As we have journeyed along the Grace Pathway, I have pointed out many of these areas where Christians might disagree with each other. The important thing is to form our own positions, learn them well, apply them to our lives, and be respectful toward those of other positions.

The simple fact is that God works through all biblically-based theological systems as long as His people turn to Him in faith, trust, and a devotion to Scripture. We are not interested in Christians fighting Christians!

One prominent Bible scholar, J.I. Packer, has done us a favor by outlining three major bible-based views on sanctification. He calls them Augustinianism, Wesleyan Perfectionism, and Keswick Teaching.[2]

I would like to simplify these positions:

---

1. Sanctification by our effort, aided by God.

This is the Augustinian view of sanctification, traceable back to St. Augustine, an early church mastermind.

Under this view, we work hard at our holiness. We strive to be like Christ, we plug in to church, fellowship, service, prayer, and Scripture. We strive to obey God. All the while, we must understand that all our striving and efforts are empowered by God Himself, and we give Him all the credit.

As a central Scripture, advocates of this view might remind you to "work out your own salvation, with fear and trembling" even as you believe that "God is working in you" (Phillipians 2:12,13).

2. Sanctification by a special, "second blessing" work of grace.

This view is called Wesleyan Perfectionism and has its

roots in John Wesley's teaching. Wesley was a preacher and church leader i the 18th century.

Under this view, a person is saved and justified at the beginning of the new life with God, and then has a second special experience with God some time later.

In this second experience—which they can feel and usually remember—God is said to dramatically break the power of sin in their lives. This leads to a life of virtual sinlessness, and perfect love for God and others. This view is called "perfectionism" and "entire sanctification."

This experience is usually brought about when you seek God intensely, and give yourself wholly and unreservedly to Him.

As a central Scripture, advocates of this view might point to 1 John 3:9: "Whoever has been born of God does not sin, for His seed remains in him; and he cannot sin, because he has been born of God," suggesting that being born of God, in this verse, reaches beyond salvation to sanctification.

3. Sanctification by grace through faith.

This view is called Keswick Sanctification (pronounced *kezzik*, the w is silent). It is named after a Bible conference grounds in England where this teaching became extremely influential and spread throughout the world.

Under this view, sanctification is as much a work of God in your life as was salvation. Did you work or strive for salvation? No. It was a gift of grace, through faith. Must you work and strive for sanctification? No. It is a gift of grace, through faith.

Some versions of this view suggest an effortless sanctification. They compare it to a divine elevator, lifting you up to heights of victorious Christian living, without you breaking a sweat.

Advocates of this view will point to the simple instruction, "As you have therefore received Christ Jesus the Lord, so walk in Him" (Colossians 2:6). Notice the word "as." It's telling us we receive sanctification in the same as we received salvation.

How did you receive Jesus at salvation? By grace, through faith. How, therefore, will you walk in Him for sanctification? By grace, through faith.

All of these views on sanctification can be developed from Scripture, so we are respectful of each one. Each has a variety of modifications made by influential teachers through the years.

As we grow mature in the Lord, it is important for us to understand that reasonable Christians have different opinions on various teachings in Scripture. It is okay for us to disagree, respectfully, and with grace. Each one of us must wrestle with Scripture and come to our own conclusions. This is healthy.

Each view on sanctification has strengths and weaknesses. Packer analyzes their pros and cons. He lands on view number one, sanctification by our effort, aided by God.

As I have studied Scripture, the strongest case can be made for view number three, sanctification by grace through faith. I will make one crucial modification to traditional Keswick teaching, however. The burden is on me to make my case. The joyful burden is on you to study it out and reach your own conclusions.

Here's my modification. I don't believe a holy life is effortless. We are not to be passive passengers on God's sanctification elevator. I believe a holy life is a mighty struggle.

But it is not the struggle most Christians think it is. Most Christians think their primary struggle is against sin. Fight the fight against sin. Wage war against sin and temptation in your life.

Sermons and books and exhortations are flung at Christians all the time, telling us to fight against sin, and to do the right thing.

That makes sense.

But...

What if fighting sin all the time is fighting the wrong battle? Let's go deeper into Scripture. Then, we will come back to the precise nature of our struggle in chapter five.

---

1. We studied the wonderful truth of Eternal Security in *Secure Forever*, Grace Pathway milestone 2.1.
2. J. I. Packer, *Keep In Step With the Spirit*, (F.H. Revell) 1984.

THE PROCESS OF SANCTIFICATION

> I have been crucified with Christ; it is no longer I who live, but Christ lives in me; and the life which I now live in the flesh I live by faith in the Son of God, who loved me and gave Himself for me. (Galatians 2:20)

Picture a gigantic, pollution-free power plant, humming along quietly. The plant produces far more power than required.

All a customer has to do is simply plug in to the power.

Our gracious Father has supplied us with three tightly connected power plants. These power plants enable us to both live and share our faith.

First, let's identify those power plants. Then we'll make sure we know how to plug in.

POWER PLANT 1: CHRIST IN YOU

The great secret of sanctifying power is Christ Himself. Christ in you.

In your very first step on the Grace Pathway — that glorious moment when God saved you — Christ Himself came to live inside you.

We will never fully understand all that this means. In fact, the Bible calls Christ's indwelling a "mystery" —"To them God willed to make known what are the riches of the glory of this mystery among the Gentiles: which is Christ in you, the hope of glory" (Colossians 1:27).

Let's agree we will never fully comprehend the mystery of what it means to have Christ in us.

Even so, every Christian should ask, "If Christ lives in me, what's He doing there?"

Answer: He is being Himself.

Jesus is living His life in and through you.

That's why Paul could say, "It is no longer I who live..." meaning, it's not just me anymore.

If you were to look at me, you might see a guy named Bill. But I'm not just Bill anymore. For the rest of forever, I am Bill plus Jesus.

Bill plus Zero no longer exists. "It is no long I (alone) who live." That identity was done away with the moment I was saved and joined to Jesus.

A new identity came into being. Bill plus Jesus.

"It is no longer I (alone) who lives, but Christ lives in me."

The same goes for you too, if you are saved. You are [insert your name here] plus Jesus, now and forevermore.

That is the real you. That is the true you. That is deepest you, and actually the only you.

Christ is in you! That means that the secret of sanctification is not *imitation*, it is *habitation*. You in Christ, and Christ in you.

> — THE SECRET OF SANCTIFICATION IS NOT IMITATION, IT IS HABITATION.

Why is Christ in you?

Not to make you a clone.

Not to make you a mindless robot.

Not to make you religious.

Christ came into you to make you YOU, your truest self, with all the color added.

He came to unbury your personality. And within your personality, to embed His own character, His own love, His own joy, and His own holiness.

As God sanctifies you, He makes you more like Christ. Actually, we should refine that thought a bit.

As God sanctifies you, Christ Himself lives more and more through you, with His character, love, holiness, and joy.

He is the power plant!

How do you plug in?

"And the life which I now live in the flesh (my human life on earth), I live by faith in the Son of God..."

Faith.

Faith is how you plug in.

Hold that thought.

POWER PLANT 2: GOD'S WORD IN YOU

In one of the most beautiful moments in the life of Christ, Jesus is found praying for us. For His Church, His people.

This is often called His High Priestly Prayer, and is recorded in John 17, the whole chapter.

Deep within this prayer, Jesus reveals one of the great secrets of sanctifying power.

> "Sanctify them by Your truth. Your word is truth." (John 17:17)

You can't live like Christ unless you think like Christ. And you can't think like Christ without the constant intake of God's Word.

Why?

Reason One is because it is in the pages of the Word that you enjoy companionship with God. This is often called fellowship, communion, or community with God. When company comes to visit, you spend time in your kitchen or living room. When you come to visit God, you spend time in his Word.

Reason Two is because when you take in the Word of God, you don't just take in information, you also take in power.

God's power.

Divine power.

Sanctifying power.

Miraculous power.

Think of the Bible as a power plant. Every verse, every promise, every teaching, every doctrine, every story, every command, every truth of Scripture goes inside of you like a little, radioactive, pellet of divine goodness and energy.

Jesus said so.

He prayed so. He prayed that God himself would sanctify you by means of the Word of God.

The whole Grace Pathway is based on this simple truth: continual growth in the Word of God is a non-negotiable essential for our growth in sanctification.

In Acts 20:32, Paul says that the Word has the power to *edify* or *build up* a child of God.

Where is the power?

In the Word.

What should we do about that?

Get the Word inside of us!

Every Christian has Christ within — power plant number one.

But not every Christian has God's Word within — power plant number two, unfortunately.

So blow the dust off that Bible of yours. Read it. Pay attention to sermons. Attend those Bible studies. And read more and more books like this one.

A worn out Bible is the emblem of a Christlike Christian.

But does that mean we are to be a bunch of brainiacs, with giant heads full of theology, and shriveled up hearts devoid of love?

Of course not.

God's Word reveals a perfect recipe for sanctification.

For every cup of Scripture, add a teaspoon of faith.

Because without faith, all that knowledge you're pouring into your brain just puffs you up (1 Corinthians 8:1). But as you learn and believe and apply scriptural truth, God changes your heart. Christ's love and life shines through.

> For indeed the gospel was preached to us as well as to them; but the word which they heard

did not profit them, not being mixed with faith in those who heard it. (Hebrews 4:2)

But the very moment you start adding faith to your knowledge, that's when the mystery of sanctification happens. More on faith in a moment.

POWER PLANT 3: GOD'S SPIRIT IN YOU

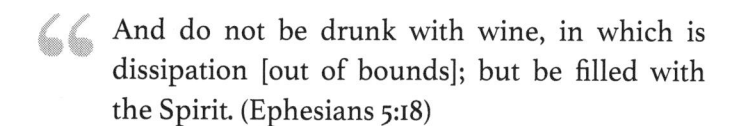

> And do not be drunk with wine, in which is dissipation [out of bounds]; but be filled with the Spirit. (Ephesians 5:18)

Just as the Spirit of God energized the human life of Christ, so the same Spirit energizes your life too.[1]

In 1 Corinthians 2, Paul lays out three kinds of people. I will stick with the traditional terms used to translate the words in this passage of Scripture.

1. *The Natural Person:* this is a person who is not saved. They have not finished Milestone One of the Grace Pathway (1 Corinthians 2:14). It is impossible for them to go deep with God because they do not possess the Holy Spirit in their lives.

2. *The Spiritual Person:* this is a person who is both saved and living day by day in the power of the Holy Spirit (v. 15). This person has "discernment" in their lives, no matter what situation they face (in "all things").

3. *The Carnal Person:* this is a person who is saved, but who is not living day by day in the power of the Holy Spirit (3:1-3). This person is dominated by their instincts, habits, and

philosophies of their pre-saved life. The Bible calls this approach to life "the flesh" and a person dominated by this approach "carnal."

Yes, the carnal person is saved. Yes, they are beloved of God. Yes, they are going to heaven and will enjoy the eternal feast of grace.

But in this life, they are stuck at the kiddie table. They are gobbling down chicken fingers and French fries while the wonders of divine grace are being enjoyed at the table set for grown ups.

> And I, brethren, could not speak to you as to spiritual people but as to carnal, as to babes in Christ. I fed you with milk and not with solid food; for until now you were not able to receive it, and even now you are still not able; for you are still carnal. For where there are envy, strife, and divisions among you, are you not carnal and behaving like mere men? (1 Corinthians 3:1-3)

Paul is writing to a bunch of crabby babies. They are carnal Christians, wasting the glories of grace on whining about their lives and getting into petty squabbles with each other.

His whole goal is to get them to make an all-important shift.

What is that shift?

From being Carnal Christians to being Spiritual Christians.

That is the same goal I have in writing this book, and, actually, in this whole Grace Pathway series.

God wants us to be filled with the Spirit (Ephesians 5:18).

He wants us to walk in the Spirit (Galatians 5:16, 25).

He wants us to shift from a carnal life to a spiritual life, living day by day under the influence of the Holy Spirit, rather than under the influence of wine, appetites, culture, peer pressure, the spirit of the age, "doctrines of demons" or any other power.

The Filling of the Holy Spirit is the third power plant of our sanctification (1 Corinthians 6:11).

Think of it.

You have both Christ in you and the Holy Spirit in you.

These two indwellings are related, but distinct.

Christ in you provides the aim and content of your sanctification. You are to be like Him. Jesus sets the standard. He points the compass north.

The Holy Spirit in you provides the power of your sanctification. As He empowered Christ in His earthly life, so He empowers you. He gives you victory. He gives you supernatural power to be Christlike. He gives you an ability to love people who are hard to love, to make choices of grace and truth a carnal Christian would never make.

This is why it is so important to be filled with the Spirit, hour by hour and day by day.

How?

How can you be filled with God's Spirit?

Ask Him.

Just ask and He will fill you. "Dear God, I have a thing happening here. Fill me with your Spirit so that I can reflect the character of Christ. Amen."

> "If you then, being evil, know how to give good gifts to your children, how much more will your

heavenly Father give the [power of the] Holy Spirit to those who ask Him!" (Luke 11:13)

If you have *grieved the Spirit* by your sins, then confess your sins to God, and move on in your life (Ephesians 4:30 and 1 John 1:9).

If you have *quenched the Spirit* by your stubbornness against God and His truth, then yield your heart to Him, and submit your life to God, and move on (1 Thessalonians 5:19 and Romans 6:13 with James 4:7).

Whenever, wherever, and as often as you bring your sins and guilt back to the Cross, when you submit your heart to God, and just ask, the Holy Spirit will fill you.

You will not necessarily feel anything different. Different Christians have different viewpoints on the emotions and feelings of the Spirit's filling.

However, almost all will agree with this truth: *there is no official feeling of the power of God.*

You might feel excited. You might feel tired. You might feel afraid. You might feel strong, or weak. Energized or blah. Happy or sad. Or you might feel nothing at all.

At the end of the day, how you feel doesn't matter.

When you ask God to fill you with His Spirit, He does. Immediately. Instantly. Invisibly.

Believe Him. Take Him by faith, and move boldly toward whatever test lies ahead, trusting that God will be all you need and more in that moment.

Just as with Christ in you, and God's Word in you, it is faith that plugs you into the power of God's Spirit in you.

Faith.

Let's talk about that kind of faith right now.

1. The Spirit energized: Christ's conception (Luke 1:35); his resistance in temptation (Matthew 4:1); his ministry (Luke 4:18); his driving out of demons (Matthew 12:28); his sacrificial death (Hebrews 9:14); his resurrection (Romans 8:11). Christ was and is both fully human and fully divine. In his human nature, he relied on the power of the Holy Spirit, just as we can today.

THE STRUGGLE OF SANCTIFICATION

At the end of chapter four, I suggested that the main struggle in our lives is not what most Christians think it is.

I said that our primary battle is not a fight against sin.

I also said that a life of sanctified holiness—the life of our dreams, the life that reflects Christ, the life that activates all our marvelous potentials—is not effortless.

A holy life is a mighty struggle.

But just what is that struggle?

It is not simply a struggle against sin.

It is not mainly a fight to overcome temptation.

It is not mainly the struggle to be a better Christian, to do more good deeds, or to work harder for Christ

It is not simply the effort to imitate Christ.

What, then, is the struggle?

Faith.

The main struggle is the struggle of faith. To believe God. To believe Him in the heat of battle. To believe His Word against all odds, and against all that your eyes can see.

Faith is a mighty struggle.

Win the battle of faith, and all your other victories will fall into place.

Faith IS the victory (1 John 5:4).

I would rather have you struggle to trust God than struggle to defeat sin. Both are part of God's plan, but faith is the main thing. Faith is the gigantic switch that turns on the power of heaven in your life.

Christ in you. God's Word in you. God's Spirit in you. The pulsating power of each one flows along the channel of faith.

The presence of faith does not mean the absence of fear. Faith does not erase your emotions. Faith does not supercharge you with superpowers. It does not make you courageous or invincible.

You might have faith, and still feel angry, disappointed, questioning, nervous, and ready to quit. You might still feel doubts.

Faith is not a shield of invincibility you psych yourself into.

Faith simply means believing that what God has said is true, enough to act like it. Trust his promises and his Word no matter what your emotions say.

Do you have a scary interview ahead of you?

Stand tall, walk into the room, and act as if God is with you. Tell yourself He's got this thing under control. Even if your heart is pounding, even if your mouth is dry, believe that God will help you and keep moving forward. That's faith.

Do you have a big, juicy temptation staring you in the face?

Sometimes, faith means getting out of the situation as much as you possibly can. Do not put yourself into the position of temptation if it's at all possible.

For example, the Bible says, "Flee sexual immorality..." (1

Corinthians 6:18). It doesn't say to stand there and negotiate. If it's an area of weakness for you, true faith runs away.

Sanctification is not only about overcoming sin, it is about having the wisdom to stay far, far away from temptations that routinely overcome you — "the sin which so easily ensnares us" (Hebrews 12:1).

Yes, we believe that God can do anything in our lives.

At the same time we recognize that there are deeply rooted patterns and addictions in our lives that require us to take decisive actions of avoidance.

Never needlessly expose yourself to temptations.

That's faith too.

Faith means believing the wisdom of God and acting accordingly.

Which leaves one final question in our quest for holiness: How do we strengthen our faith?

FAITH WITH MUSCLE

Faith itself is simple. You can exercise faith at any time in any circumstance. In any trouble. In any heartbreak. In any temptation. There has never been a moment in your life when the simple choice of faith is beyond your reach.

All it requires is saying, Lord, I believe.

> No temptation has overtaken you except such as is common to man; but God is faithful, who will not allow you to be tempted beyond what you are able, but with the temptation will also make the way of escape, that you may be able to bear it. (1 Corinthians 10:13)

But just because faith is simple does not mean it is easy.

This is why we need to put some muscle on our faith. How?

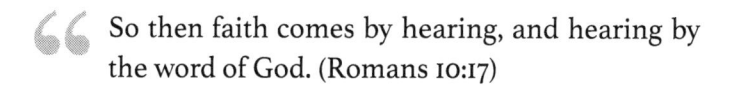

> So then faith comes by hearing, and hearing by the word of God. (Romans 10:17)

Translation: grow up in grace and knowledge so you can pack some muscle on your faith.

Because faith is the magic ingredient that plugs you into the sanctifying power of God. That is when you exhibit grace under pressure. That is when you love those who least deserve it. That is when you trust God against all odds. That is when you make the hard choices that are holy and can work against you, but you're leaving the outcomes to God. That is when you make the faith-based choices that overcome temptation or avoid it all together.

Anybody can trust God in good times.

But it takes a level of maturity and growth to trust Him in hard times. Hopefully, the whole Grace Pathway is developing that spiritual muscle in you!

This is when the glory of Christ's holiness and grace can really shine through the most unlikely vessels like us.

> For whatever is born of God overcomes the world. And this is the victory that has overcome the world — our faith. (1 John 5:4)

Whatever is born of God overcomes the world. What does that mean? It means that you, walking in your new nature that has been born of God, living in the power of regeneration, and exercising even the tiniest faith, will achieve monumental victories over the temptations of the world.

Faith is the victory.

Trust God and obey Him. Trust God and move forward. Put your faith in him and engage the enemy, believe God's promises and take the test. Speak the hard truth, take the risk.

Faith is the biggest struggle in our Christian lives, yes.

But faith is also the victory, every single time.

Your job is faith; God's job is outcomes.

Every time you win the struggle of faith, all your other victories fall into place.

THE RESULTS OF SANCTIFICATION

The Bible portrays God's people as a basically unruly lot. A truly sanctified life is hard to come by. In the epic of Scripture, holiness seems to be the exception rather than the rule.

But when you do find those characters whose faith shines in difficult times, you also find that the world around them is changed.

Joseph kept faith with God, walked in holiness, and saved his world from famine and death. He shines as an everlasting witness to the gospel of grace.

Esther kept faith with God, walked in courage, and delivered her people from holocaust. Her testimony shines as an endless beacon to a bold faith in an illimitable God.

Ruth kept faith with God, walked in self-giving grace, and rescued her mother-in-law from poverty and starvation—only then to find herself unexpectedly inserted into God's cosmic plan of redemption. Her faith in times of trouble radiates an enduring summons to a God of all grace.

An old-time evangelist famously said,

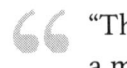

> "The world has yet to see what God can do with a man fully consecrated to him. By God's help, I aim to be that man."
>
> — DWIGHT L. MOODY, 1800S

The humblest woman or man, walking in sanctification, is a death-dealing blow to the devil's lies. Our world, trapped in darkness, urgently needs to see sanctified Christians.

Set aside all the techniques and strategies of the church. Set aside all the politicking and agendas. Set aside social media posts and advertising and protests and boycotts. Even set aside organizations for prayer and spiritual warfare.

Until Jesus comes, the greatest force for good on planet earth is the humblest child of God, first filled with grace and truth, and then living for the Master.

The world has no argument against our love, our wisdom, our self-sacrifice, and our gospel when we first live, and second, share, our faith.

Holiness. Love. Joy. Courage. Loving words and actions. The character of Christ living through you in your everyday routines. Power over temptation. Choosing against sin.

It's your choice. All of it. You hold the keys.

The final step in living a sanctified life is simply to tell God you want it.

CONSECRATION

It is no mistake that a life of sanctification has not been a major theme in the Grace Pathway until now. I know it's coming relatively late in the discipleship journey.

This is because when sanctification is brought in before grace is established, it turns into legalism and self-effort.

Before you ever even think of dedicating your life to God, it is all-important that you realize His infinite dedication to you first. That has been the pattern of the Grace Pathway.

We don't serve God for blessing; we serve Him from blessing.

All good works, all Christian service, and all holiness in your life can only exist within the overflow of grace in your heart.

That is why, for six books, I have emphasized what God has done for you.

Grace first. Grace as the foundation.

Now we're ready to talk about what you do for God.

Consecration is an act — a decision, a moment, what some call a "crisis experience" — in which you tell God that you intend to live a life of grace-powered holiness.

> I beseech you therefore, brethren, by the mercies of God, that you present your bodies a living sacrifice, holy, acceptable to God, which is your reasonable service. (Romans 12:1)

In grace, God has said to you, "Christian, I am yours."

In sanctification by grace, you can now say, "God, I am Yours."

Have you ever presented "your body"—and with your body, your whole self—to God as a living sacrifice?

This is not the way of salvation, but of sanctification. And the act or moment is called consecration.

God I am Yours. My life is in Your hands. By grace, I will live for You. By grace, I will follow You anywhere. I will stand on Your Truth. I will trust Your Heart even when I do not understand Your Ways.

My life of service to You, Lord, is an enduring "thank You" for all Your amazing grace.

God, I dedicate my life to You.

By the mercies of God—in view of the oceans of grace and depths of Calvary Love—I tell You, I am Yours forever.

This is consecration.

This is dedication, or maybe rededication, of your life to God.

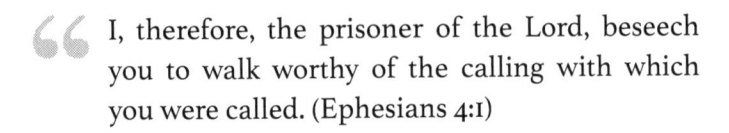

> I, therefore, the prisoner of the Lord, beseech you to walk worthy of the calling with which you were called. (Ephesians 4:1)

May I lovingly encourage you right now to consecrate your life to the Lord?

Tell Him it is your intention to walk in faith.

Tell Him your desire to live a life of grace-powered holiness and truth.

Tell Him your ambition to "walk worthy of the calling with which you were called."

Declare your desire that Christ may be seen in you, in the most everyday affairs of your life.

Declare your grace-filled determination to conquer patterns of sin in your life by God's own power, that you might walk in victory.

Ask God to use you mightly for Christ and His Gospel.

Declare yourself to be a servant of the Great King.

And then add this confession: *God, I do not have within myself the power to do any of these things. So the power must come from You. By Christ in me, Your Word in me, and Your Spirit in me, make me the person of faith You know I can become. Amen.*

It's a scary thing to put Jesus first in your life.

But it's the most adventurous, joyful, and meaningful life you will ever live.

One man, one woman, consecrated to Jesus Christ, can literally change their world.

This is what you were created for.

And this is what a lost and dying world most desperately needs to see.

THE FRUIT OF SANCTIFICATION

Every good thing in the life of a Christian is the fruit of God's effort through the sanctifying presence of Christ in you. If there is one molecule of goodness in your life, Jesus gets the credit. He is the one worthy of praise. None of us can boast.

Christ himself is reproducing his own character and life in you.

Imagine Christianity as a beautiful fruit tree. Salvation is the root. Spiritual growth — edification, sanctification — is the trunk. And the character of Christ expressed through you is the fruit. What does that fruit look like?

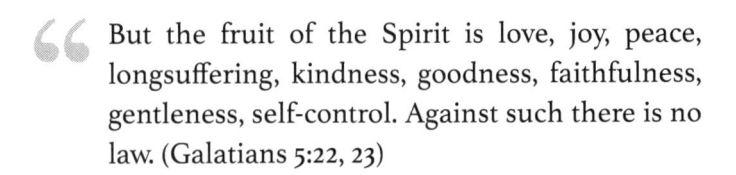

> But the fruit of the Spirit is love, joy, peace, longsuffering, kindness, goodness, faithfulness, gentleness, self-control. Against such there is no law. (Galatians 5:22, 23)

Who doesn't want that kind of life? You can't put a price tag on love, joy, peace, and the rest. Yet this is the awesome promise of God to every believer who will walk by faith, grow mature, and let the life of Christ flow.

As part of the Grace Pathway, we will highlight two aspects of the fruit of sanctification — generosity and the one anothers.

GENEROSITY

One of the surest signs of a growth in a Christian's life is a spirit of generosity. Biblically speaking, the main expression of this spirit of generosity is joyful financial support of your home church.

> On every Lord's Day, each of you should put aside some amount of money in relation to what you have earned and save it for this offering. Don't wait until I get there and then try to collect it all at once. (1 Corinthians 16:2, NLT)

The Lord's Day is the first day of the week, Sunday. This Scripture shows us the practice of the early Christians in giving an offering in church when they met on Sundays. Today, churches may meet on different days of the week, but the principle remains the same. Put aside some amount of money, corresponding to what you have earned, and save it for the offering.

Your heart's attitude is very important in this matter.

> So let each one give as he purposes in his heart, not grudgingly or of necessity; for God loves a cheerful giver. (2 Corinthians 9:7)

When Scripture says that our giving should not be done

"grudgingly" or "of necessity," this is God's reminder that generous giving to your church is always a result of grace. Guilt, shame, duty, and obligation are terrible motivations for giving. But when your heart is full of grace and truth, and when you overflow with gratitude to God for your amazing salvation, and for the riches of grace in your life, it is easy to say thank you to God by joyfully and generously giving to support the ministry of your church.

Every offering is another chance to say thank you to God for your salvation in Christ. The deeper your appreciation for that salvation, the more cheerful and joyful your giving will be.

The Bible also sets this spirit of generosity within the concept of *stewardship*. In Scripture, a steward is the manager of a household. The owner entrusts their property to the steward, and the steward manages that property for the benefit and pleasure of the owner.

God is the owner. He owns all things.

Every single resource, asset, blessing, and treasure you have in your life has come from God. He is the owner. This is a difficult, and mature, way of looking at things. All your "stuff" is from God and for God. Everything you have is His.

So what does that make you?

A steward.

What does God expect of stewards? "Moreover it is required in stewards that one be found faithful" (1 Corinthians 4:2). You might worry that you can't be faithful enough to please God. Don't worry, Christ is faithful, he is living in and through you, and if you keep on growing and walking in faith, his faithfulness will shine through.

Say it to yourself over and over again: *I am a steward of God's stuff. I manage God's property for his benefit and pleasure*

> As each one has received a gift, minister it to one another, as good stewards of the manifold grace of God. (1 Peter 4:10)

If you consider everything you own as God's property, including your money, it becomes easier to return to him a portion of what he has given you when the offering plate goes by. When you can say, "God, all I am, and all I have, is yours," then it feels like a privilege to express generosity in the offering at your church.

Another aspect of generosity and giving is that we are to feed the church that feeds our souls. In other words, you may find a lot of good outlets for your generosity — helping the poor and oppressed, providing clean water in third world countries, and helping solve problems of homelessness and hunger. These are wonderful projects to support with our money.

However, the first place we should support is our own church. The principle is that we should not starve the ministry that nurtures our spirit in order to feed other ministries, however good they might be.

> For the Scripture says, "You shall not muzzle an ox while it treads out the grain," and, "The laborer is worthy of his wages." (1 Timothy 5:18)

The ox is your pastor and your church. The muzzle prevents the ox from eating as it is treading or working. The muzzle represents anything that would "starve" your pastor and church from eating and living even as they are busy serving you. So the conclusion is to financially support the church and pastor that is busy laboring on your behalf... and to do so with a spirit of thankfulness and joy. "The laborer [your pastors and your church] is worthy of his wages."

Any giving to other ministries is best when it is given above and beyond your giving to your own church. Hopefully, your church is already doing many of the social ministries you feel motivated to support!

It's always good to ask your pastor or other church leaders about how they view giving and generosity. That way you can go with the flow of your church.

One final aspect of generosity is that we technically don't give our money to the church, we give it to the Lord. We let it go into his hands. This turns giving into worship.

> Give to the LORD the glory due His name; Bring an offering, and come into His courts. (Psalm 96:8)

May God give you joy as the fruit of generosity is increasingly displayed in your life.

THE ONE ANOTHERS

Perhaps the most important fruit of sanctification is love. The Bible has an awesome way of helping us understand what Christ's love looks like as it flows through us. This is through what is called "the one anothers" of Scripture.

Probably the easiest way to understand this is by simply listing them.

---

1. "Be at peace with each other." (Mark 9:50)
2. "Wash one another's feet." (John 13:14)

3. "Love one another..." (John 13:34, 15:12, Romans 13:8, multiple Scriptures)
4. "Be devoted to one another in brotherly love..." (Romans 12:10)
5. "Honor one another above yourselves. (Romans 12:10)
6. "Live in harmony with one another..." (Romans 12:16)
7. "Stop passing judgment on one another." (Romans 14:13)
8. "Accept one another, then, just as Christ accepted you..." (Romans 15:7)
9. "Instruct one another." (Romans 15:14)
10. "Greet one another with a holy kiss..." (Romans 16:16, I Corinthians 16:20, II Corinthians 13:12)
11. "When you come together to eat, wait for each other." (I Cor. 11:33)
12. "Have equal concern for each other." (I Corinthians 12:25)
13. "Serve one another in love." (Galatians 5:13)
14. "Let us not become conceited, provoking and envying each other." (Galatians 5:26)
15. "Carry each other's burdens..." (Galatians 6:2)
16. "Be patient, bearing with one another in love." (Ephesians 4:2)
17. "Be kind and compassionate to one another..." (Ephesians 4:32)
18. "Forgiving each other..." (Ephesians 4:32)
19. "Speak to one another with psalms, hymns and spiritual songs." (Ephesians 5:19)
20. "Submit to one another out of reverence for Christ." (Ephesians 5:21)

21. "In humility consider others better than yourselves." (Philippians 2:3)
22. "Do not lie to each other…" (Colossians 3:9)
23. "Bear with each other…" (Colossians 3:13)
24. "Forgive whatever grievances you may have against one another." (Colossians 3:13)
25. "Teach…[one another]" (Colossians 3:16)
26. "Admonish one another (Colossians 3:16)
27. "Make your love increase and overflow for each other." (I Thessalonians 3:12)
28. "Encourage each other…"(I Thessalonians 4:18, I Thessalonians 5:11, Hebrews 10:25)
29. "Build each other up…" (I Thessalonians 5:11)
30. "Encourage one another daily…" Hebrews 3:13)
31. "Spur one another on toward love and good deeds." (Hebrews 10:24)
32. "Do not slander one another." (James 4:11)
33. "Don't grumble against each other…" (James 5:9)
34. "Confess your sins to each other…" (James 5:16)
35. "Pray for each other." (James 5:16)
36. "Love one another deeply, from the heart." (I Peter 3:8)
37. "Live in harmony with one another…" (I Peter 3:8)
38. "Love each other deeply…" (I Peter 4:8)
39. "Offer hospitality to one another without grumbling." (I Peter 4:9)
40. "Each one should use whatever gift he has received to serve others…" (I Peter 4:10)
41. "Clothe yourselves with humility toward one another…"(I Peter 5:5)[1]

God's purposes seem pretty clear. Living your faith means loving the family of faith along with the world for whom Christ died.

It's easy to look at these one anothers as a to-do list. If that were the case, all of this would be an incredible burden.

It is liberating, however, and much more biblical, to view these one anothers as the fruit of God's work in your life. Put together, these one anothers paint a portrait of the life of Christ.

Wouldn't it be wonderful if your life began to resemble his life more and more?

That is the promise and blessing of sanctification. It is the heart and soul of living your faith. The one anothers are the fruit of God's work in you.

And it will become an unbeatable argument for God when you go out and share your faith with a lost and confused generation.

---

1. This list is modified from the Small Group Churches website, retrieved July 13, 2020 from https://www.smallgroupchurches.com/the-59-one-anothers-of-the-bible/

SHARING YOUR FAITH

THE NATURE OF EVANGELISM

Living your faith and sharing your faith go hand in hand. As the truth of God's grace transforms your life, the gospel of God's salvation rings true in your testimony.

There is nobody who works harder at the salvation of lost people than God Himself. God is the Great Evangelist.

If there are people in your life who don't know Christ, God is witnessing to them already.

He's the shepherd who goes after the lost sheep.

He's the host who chases down the last stray guest.

He's the physician who searches for the spiritually wounded and morally sick.

He's the Father who never gives up on His prodigal daughter or son.

He's the friend who sticks closer than a brother.

He's the Light for those who wander in darkness.

He's the Sun of Righteousness for those trapped in perpetual night.

He's the Bright Morning Star pointing the wayfarer home.

> What man of you, having a hundred sheep, if he loses one of them, does not leave the ninety-nine in the wilderness, and go after the one which is lost until he finds it? And when he has found it, he lays it on his shoulders, rejoicing. And when he comes home, he calls together his friends and neighbors, saying to them, "Rejoice with me, for I have found my sheep which was lost!" (Luke 15:4-6)

If you love somebody who doesn't know Jesus, God loves them more.

If you worry over them, God worries more — in His own perfect way.

If you labor for their salvation — and you should — God labors more. He promised.

God loves your family more than you do. He loves your city, your county, your region, and your nation more than you do.

God wants lost people found, and folded into the family of faith. He never rests in that endeavor.

Do realize, however, God is a gentleman. He will never force a person to receive Christ and His gift of salvation against their will.

But He will bring circumstances to bear that bring them face to face with Christ and with their need for a Savior. That's His love at work.

God is working, all the time, to effect the salvation of every single lost person you know and don't know.

Jesus said, "And I, if I am lifted up from the earth, will draw all men to Myself" (John 12:32, NAS95). He's doing that right now.

WHAT IS EVANGELISM?

Evangelism is the ceaseless work of God in drawing sinners to Himself through the proclamation of the Gospel by Christians who are living and sharing their faith.

God loves lost people and wants them found.

You have probably noticed that God didn't sweep you into heaven the minute you were saved. He left you here in this fallen world for many reasons. One of the main reasons is so you can participate in evangelism.

> — EVANGELISM IS THE CEASELESS WORK OF GOD IN DRAWING SINNERS TO HIMSELF THROUGH THE PROCLAMATION OF THE GOSPEL BY CHRISTIANS WHO ARE LIVING AND SHARING THEIR FAITH.

The Church—the collection of all true believers in the world—is God's chosen instrument for evangelism in every generation.

It's not by accident that we have combined *living your faith* (sanctification) and *sharing your faith* (evangelism) in one book.

In one sense, evangelism is sanctification's high point. The Grace Pathway's final milestone is God Uses You, and evangelistic impact is the greatest way in which that happens.

> Now then, we are ambassadors for Christ, as though God were pleading through us: we implore you on Christ's behalf, be reconciled to God. (2 Corinthians 5:20)

You are an Ambassador of Christ! That's amazing! What a privilege! What an exalted rank!

You stand in for Him. You speak for Him. You represent Him. God trusts *you* with His Gospel message in this fallen world.

What is the core of our ambassadorship? It is "as though God were pleading through us..."

Let that sink in.

God is pleading through you.

Almighty God is using *you* — your voice, your love, your intellect, your actions — to "implore" sinners "on Christ's behalf."

What are we imploring sinners to do?

"Be reconciled to God."

This takes us all the way back to Milestone Three, where we studied the Cross of Christ. All those incredible doctrines of justification, propitiation, redemption, and the rest — they all add up to one beautiful moment: reconciliation with God.

Your mission, should you decide to accept it, is to fulfill your Ambassadorship well.

In the next few chapters, we will learn how to do just that.

PRE-EVANGELISM

As an Ambassador of heaven, you have one main message. That message is the Gospel. In the first three books in the Grace Pathway, we laid out the Gospel and made it plain.

Evangelism happens when the Gospel is communicated and the Holy Spirit is enabling the hearer to understand it.

One of the most incredible moments in your life will be that glorious day when you see with your very own eyes a person cross the line of faith and be born into God's family forever.

That is the greatest miracle on earth, and, by getting involved in evangelism, you are part of it.

We can think of evangelism in three stages:

---

1. PRE-EVANGELISM

Pre-evangelism includes everything we do to deepen relationships, and gain credibility with the people in our lives. It also includes everything God does to prepare a person for the Gospel.

Living your faith (sanctification) is part of pre-evangelism, because it gives you extra credibility when you share your faith (evangelism).

It's hard for lost people to argue with the Gospel when it's coming from the lips of one of the most loving and generous people in their lives.

So, you be that person.

BUT... even if you're not that person, the Gospel message still has a power all its own. Christ has more attracting power than we give Him credit for. The Gospel communicated is "the power of God," whether our lives back it up well or not (Romans 1:16). The Spirit of God supplies His own energy to our Gospel presentations, even if we are imperfect in our lives or words.

What I'm saying is this: you don't have to wait for super-high levels of sanctification before you start evangelism, especially for newer Christians.

However, in pre-evangelism, a few things happen.

a) God softens a person's heart.

He begins plowing up the hard soil to receive the seed of the Gospel (Matthew 13:18, ff.). There is less resistance. More openness to conversation. Reduced cynicism. A softening of the heart and an increased willingness to listen. God is an expert at bringing circumstances into a person's life that will make that person look up, and think of Him.

b) Misconceptions are straightened out.

Most unsaved people carry a boatload of misconceptions

about Christianity and Christians. As God draws a person to Himself, He uses your life, and many other influences, to correct those misconceptions. Maybe Christians aren't that awful, and Christianity isn't as rigid as people have thought!

c) Friendships are formed.

This is because the Gospel flows most naturally across relational networks. Friendships. Families. Teams. Classrooms. These networks are described by the biblical term, *oikos* (household). This is why Paul and Silas could tell the Philippian jailer, "Believe on the Lord Jesus Christ, and you will be saved, you *and your household*" (Acts 16:31).

d) Credibility is gained.

All the good stuff Christians do in the world lends credibility to our message. Social ministry, helping those in need — these are expressions of the Gospel, but in themselves, they do not save a person. People need to hear about Christ crucified and risen again. They need to connect the dots between Christ's death and their sins. They need a summons to faith alone in Christ alone.

Any acts of kindness, any social endeavors, any good deeds that we do might open the doors to an audience. But, unless Christ is explicitly preached, people can't be genuinely saved.

The abundance of good deeds done in Jesus' name have never saved a soul. Yes, they are important and of high value. But nothing surpasses the value of finding Christ Jesus as Savior and then following Him as Lord.

e) Reality rises up.

Remember, we are talking about what happens in a person's life before they are saved, and before they receive the Gospel.

The reality is that a life without God at the core is broken. Our friends have come up with a million ways to mask that brokenness.

As God draws a person to Himself, sometimes those masks begin to fracture. Reality breaks through, and that reality can be painful, frustrating, and even ugly.

This is God holding up a mirror to show a person the corruption of their own hearts before they are reconciled to Him.

One of the best mirrors in the Bible is the Ten Commandments. The laws of God have a "convicting" power (Romans 3:20, John 16:8).

What if a person doesn't believe the Bible? What if they disagree with the Ten Commandments?

Surprisingly, it really doesn't matter.

Reality is reality, and reality rings true, whether a person wants it to, or not. When God says that a certain lifestyle is out of bounds — don't steal, don't commit adultery, don't worship other gods — then that lifestyle is bound to create pain. Count on it. That is simple reality.

God loves people too much to subsidize a life heading toward self-destruction.

One way or another, God will bring people face to face with their need of a Savior.

COME TO JESUS

Jesus explained why: "Those who are well have no need of a physician, but those who are sick" (Luke 5:31).

Until a person's moral and spiritual sickness smacks them in the face, they won't admit their need of a Savior.

Enter God's laws.

God's laws show forth two sides of the same coin: God's demands and mankind's failure. There's a huge gap between what we should be and what we are.

Sensing that gap is key to moving a person from the stage of pre-evangelism to the stage of evangelism.

You could say that pre-evangelism is God's way of making a person willing to hear the Gospel.

It's pretty common for Christians to talk about "coming to Christ." That's excellent language, as it is biblically accurate. Jesus said, "Come unto me" (Matthew 11:28, John 5:40). So we're justified when we invite our friends to "come to Jesus" and trust Him as Savior.

But there's a better picture of what happens when a person is saved.

> ...that by two immutable things, in which it is impossible for God to lie, we might have strong consolation, who have fled for refuge to lay hold of the hope set before us. (Hebrews 6:18)

A Christian is a person who has "fled for refuge" to Christ.

It's not that we simply sauntered up to Jesus one day, and casually said, "Please save me."

If we really get what it means to stand before a holy God, and what it means to be a sinner before Him, and if we really get how awesome a Savior He is, we don't just come to Jesus, we *run* to Jesus. We flee to Him for refuge. Our trust in Him is coupled with a huge sense of relief.

That doesn't mean we have to beat people over the head

with how guilty and messed up they are. A true appreciation of salvation takes time

It takes growth. It takes God's glorious Grace Pathway for us to really understand the magnitude of our salvation.

But none of that can happen until a person comes face to face with the Savior.

That's where evangelism comes in.

THREE PRINCIPLES OF EVANGELISM

There's an old saying: evangelism is one beggar telling another beggar where to find bread. I am very grateful for the people in my life who told me where to find the Bread of Life. I am thankful for the people who loved me, prayed for me, answered my questions, put up with me, and shared Christ with me.

Now, it's my turn.

And it's your turn, too.

Let's do all we can to announce to our world that a Savior has come, and His name is Jesus.

You, contributing your life to the great cause of evangelism, is one of the main goals of the Grace Pathway.

Here are three principles to guide us as we go.

---

1. Evangelism requires words.

Parents often tell their toddlers, "Use your words." Jesus wants us to use our words too.

Christians are fond of an old saying of St. Francis: "Preach the gospel at all times. If necessary, use words." The sentiment is good — that we should both live and share our faith.

But the implication is not so good, because this statement implies that words are optional when it comes to evangelism. This flies in the face of Scripture and history.

> How then shall they call on Him in whom they have not believed? And how shall they believe in Him of whom they have not heard? And how shall they hear without a preacher? (Romans 10:14)

Words are not optional. We have a Gospel message that is meant to be conveyed in words. It is meant to be preached. It is meant to be heard.

2. In evangelism, we present a precise message.

God is very clear that the Gospel message must remain unpolluted. No good works. No religious observance. No moral performance. No human effort. No element of human endeavor must cloud the crystal clear waters of saving grace.

Scripture underlines the importance of not messing around with the Gospel message:

> But even if we, or an angel from heaven, preach any other gospel to you than what we have preached to you, let him be accursed. As we have said before, so now I say again, if anyone preaches any other gospel to you than what you have received, let him be accursed. (Galatians 1:8, 9)

There is only one Gospel message, and it is focused with laser-like precision on the saving work of Christ.

The last thing I want to do is to scare you off from sharing your faith! This whole book is about helping you do that.

This verse is a warning to church leaders to make sure that when we teach and preach the Gospel, we make sure to point to Jesus Christ and His saving work, plus or minus nothing.

God is not going to be picky with you on how you present the Gospel. He loves it when you try, even if the words don't come out right. Even your feet are beautiful when you share Christ (Romans 10:15).

But let's do our best to communicate a simple and crystal clear Gospel of grace (Acts 20:24).

3. Evangelism is motivated by grace.

Every person who gets saved reduces by one the number of people in hell. To me, that's motivational. So, one motivation for evangelism is *a sense of concern.*

In my doctoral program, I wrote a major paper arguing that the existence of hell was a valid and central motive for evangelism in the early church.[1] My professor didn't like it. Not because of of how it was written, But because of my theology. My professor wasn't so sure about hell. That's a view called universalism ("all roads lead to God").

Sad to say, to strengthen universalism is to weaken evangelism.

But the Bible is clear, and the stakes could not be higher. Every person's eternal destiny hinges on the question: what did you do with Jesus? Who was He to you? Was He alone your Savior, or have you placed your hopes in something else?

> How then shall they call on Him in whom they have not believed? And how shall they believe in Him of whom they have not heard? And how shall they hear without a preacher? (Romans 10:14)

> Knowing, therefore, the terror of the Lord, we persuade men... (2 Corinthians 5:11)

If you believe that every human soul is immortal — as the Bible teaches — and if you believe that the wages of sin is death and that outside of Christ there is no hope — as the Bible also teaches — then it is impossible to possess an ounce of human compassion without wanting urgently for all people to know there is a way of escape from the wrath of God.

The growth of grace in our hearts creates this deep sense of concern for lost people.

A second motivation, also stemming from grace, is *a sense of gratitude.*

The more you understand the sacrifice Jesus made for you, and the salvation Jesus won for you, the more you want everybody you know to find the treasure you found when you found Christ.

The earliest Christians were captivated by a God of love. Paul said the "love of Christ compels us" (2 Corinthians 5:14).

The idea that "God is love" had never occurred before (1 John 4:8, 16).

His love wasn't just an abstract love — it was as real, and gritty, and bloody as an old rugged Cross. It was a self-sacrificing love. It was a demanding, costly, unparalleled love, displayed by the Son of God at Calvary.

It blew them away. They couldn't keep silent. "For we

cannot but speak the things which we have seen and heard." (Acts 4:20)

From a practical standpoint, it made no sense for the early Christians to evangelize. It cost them everything. The Gospel was hated. It was misunderstood and misrepresented.

But the earliest Christians were so overwhelmed by the love of God they couldn't help themselves.

Why do we share Christ?

We share Christ because we want everybody to find the treasure we found when we found Christ.

Now let's see exactly what our Gospel message is.

---

1. I highly recommend Michael Green's well-documented book, *Evangelism in the Early Church,* a study of the methods of motives for evangelism in the first generations after Christ.

THE GOSPEL MESSAGE

When we evangelize, we are basically communicating a packet of information. A packet of truth, so to speak.

That packet contains an irreducible minimum of very specific truths.

Scripture is super clear on these truths:

- For I determined not to know anything among you except Jesus Christ and Him crucified. (1 Corinthians 2:2)
- But God forbid that I should boast except in the cross of our Lord Jesus Christ, by whom the world has been crucified to me, and I to the world. (Galatians 6:14)
- For I delivered to you first of all that which I also received: that *Christ died for our sins* according to the Scriptures, and that He was buried, and that He rose again the third day according to the Scriptures, (1 Corinthians 15:3, 4)

The heart of the Gospel message can be communicated in five simple words. Five monosyllables: *Christ died for our sins.* This is the Gospel.

Any presentation, teaching, sermon, or invitation that does not proclaim and explain this little sentence is simply not the Gospel.

Let's break it down.

"Christ died..." —*that part is HISTORY.*

If you had been there, you would have seen this. You would have seen the beatings, seen the soldiers nail Him to the cross. You would have seen the crown of thorns. You would have heard Him cry out, "It is finished" and you would have seen Him die and breathe His last. Christ died... that event is history. But what does it mean?"

"For our sins..." —*that part is THEOLOGY.*

The backdrop to the Gospel is human sinfulness. We are messed up people in the presence of a fiercely holy God. This is a huge, humanly impossible, problem. Hopefully, you can see how this is where all our previous milestones, such as *Knowing God* and *The Cross,* come together.

Jesus died as a payment for our sins. He died in our place. This is the theology of substitutionary atonement. In theology, it is called vicarious atonement. It means that His death counts for you. God punished Him instead of punishing you. He was your scapegoat. He was your sacrifice. He was your Lamb of God to take away the sin of YOU. When Jesus died, your sins were transferred to Him and judged. The one thing that kept you from God — the stain and guilt of sin — was paid in full. Jesus demolished the barrier.

There is nothing left to do but say yes to the gift.

What is the Gospel?

The Gospel is the good news that Jesus died for your sins, and when He did that, He so completely satisfied the justice of God that you can be totally forgiven and embraced by God forever and ever, all because of Him. Therefore you are invited, called, and summoned to believe in Him and receive Him as your Savior.

So let's get mildly technical. The Gospel has two sides...

- The OBJECTIVE side of the Gospel: what Christ has already done, two thousand years ago. We can call this *the facts of the Gospel.*
- The SUBJECTIVE side of the Gospel: how a person responds to the objective side. We can call this *the invitation of the Gospel.*

So, a complete act of evangelism communicates the basic facts of the Gospel — this can take a long time, or a short time. Even as little as two minutes. Whatever it takes to help a person realize, a) they need a Savior, b) Jesus shed His blood and died to be that Savior, and c) no works, effort, performance, or religion could ever reconcile them to God. Just Jesus, crucified and risen again.

Evangelism then has a next step. In that step, we invite a person to believe in the Savior and actually be saved.

In the Grace Pathway, we have already learned a great deal about the objective side of the Gospel. In the book, *The Cross,* we dug into the wonders of all Christ did to demolish the barrier between us and God.

So now what? If Christ has objectively opened the door of salvation, exactly how do we subjectively step through?

FAITH ALONE

The only biblical response is faith or believing. What is biblical faith? Here's a simple definition.

Saving faith is claiming by personal choice and trusting exclusively in Christ and his finished work on the Cross as my only hope for salvation.

> — SAVING FAITH IS CLAIMING BY PERSONAL CHOICE AND TRUSTING EXCLUSIVELY IN CHRIST AND HIS FINISHED WORK ON THE CROSS AS MY ONLY HOPE FOR SALVATION.

Scripture again is very clear:

- In Him you also trusted, after you heard the word of truth, the Gospel of your salvation; in whom also, having believed, you were sealed with the Holy Spirit of promise, (Ephesians 1:13)
- God has appointed Him as the means of propitiation, a propitiation accomplished by the shedding of His blood, to be received and made effective in ourselves by faith. (Romans 3:25, Phil).

Salvation is by grace alone, through faith alone, in Christ alone.

Salvation happens when a person transfers all their faith from anything else to Christ. We stop believing in our religious rituals, good works, moral performance, service, self-sacrifice, or anything else, and start resting our full weight on Jesus Christ.

This transference of trust is called *repentance*. Repentance does not mean to change our lives, or to turn over a new leaf. No human effort plays any part when it comes to getting saved.

Salvation is never about changing our behavior to gain God's approval.

Repentance means to turn from all false hopes that we might trust in the One True Hope, who is Jesus (Hebrews 6:1).

When we present the Gospel, we strip away all other hopes, so that the spotlight shines exclusively on Jesus, crucified and risen again.

In the very moment a sinner believes in Jesus as Savior, they become a saint. It's truly amazing.

When you participate in evangelism, you actually get to witness the miracle of all miracles, a person being born again.

Here's a simple framework to guide your friends into declaring their faith in Christ.

TYING THE KNOT

There's a golden moment in a wedding ceremony when a couple says, "I do," and they are pronounced husband and wife. That moment is often called "Tying the Knot."

It's the definitive moment of marriage. A line is crossed. It's official. Two have become one.

So it is in salvation. In this chapter, we will learn how to Tie the Knot of salvation for our friends.

Over the years, God's people have developed many evangelistic training programs. These have been a wonderful gift to the church, and countless people have found salvation as a result of their influence.

Sometimes, these programs use "scripts" to help you guide a conversation toward spiritual things. These can be excellent tools.

Other programs use "diagnostic questions" to help clarify

where a person actually stands in relation to salvation. You may have heard these questions. They include, "If you were to die tonight, do you know for sure you would go to heaven?" And, "If God were to ask you, 'Why should I let you into my heaven,' what would you tell Him?"

All of these tools are great. I'm a big fan of any godly methods used to advance evangelism.

Our approach, however, will be based more on *principles*, than a preset formula of questions. We will seek to follow the promptings of the Holy Spirit, more than anything else.

So let's get to a simple framework of actually tying the knot.

THE ABCS OF THE GOSPEL

In the moment of faith, a person who is coming to Christ has something to admit, something to believe, and something they must choose.

These are the ABCs of the Gospel: Admit. Believe. Choose.

The simplest way to tie the knot, and to help a friend express saving faith, is to lead them through a prayer that covers the ABCs.

First, we'll explain the ABCs, and then we'll put together the prayer. Please don't feel you have to cover *everything*. That would be a mistake!

All you need is just enough talking to explain the essence of the Gospel.

Less is more.

I recommend you write these ABCs in the front cover of

your Bible, along with the Bible verse references that we'll give below.

ADMIT

When a person expresses saving faith, the first thing they should do is ADMIT they need salvation. Why? Because they have sinned.

ADMIT... Tell God that you admit you are a sinner and you need salvation.

None of us can come to God until we admit our need of a Savior.

You've got to feel thirsty before you'll drink the living waters.

You've got to feel hungry before you'll partake of the bread of life.

You've got to feel sick before you'll visit the Great Physician.

You've got to feel endangered before you'll flee for refuge to the Hope set before you.

God wants to bring us to a point of giving up, so that we flee for refuge to lay hold of the hope set before us... which is Jesus, crucified and risen again.

The good news is that all your masks can come off before God.

You don't have to play holy with Him. Come just as you are.

When the Prodigal Son returned home, he admitted his unworthiness, "Father, I have sinned against heaven and in your sight, and am no longer worthy to be called your son" (Luke 15:21,).

Whatever words, whatever terminology, whatever specific sins a person wants to confess, the key is that they acknowledge they are far from God, it's a serious problem, and it's their own fault.

Some Bible verses you might use here include:

- For all have sinned and fall short of the glory of God, (Romans 3:23)
- For the wages of sin is death, but the gift of God is eternal life in Christ Jesus our Lord. (Romans 6:23)

I suggest that you write these references in the front of your Bible.

BELIEVE

After a person admits their need of a Savior, they should tell God they BELIEVE that Christ alone is that Savior.

BELIEVE... Tell God that you BELIEVE He sent Jesus to die on the Cross to be the Savior you need.

Make sure that the core of the Gospel, "Christ died for your sins," is part of this expression of faith.

Do good works save a person? No. Just faith alone in Christ alone.

Do religious rituals save a person? No. Just faith alone in Christ alone.

Does obedience save a person? No. Just faith alone in Christ alone.

Does moral improvement, personal success, anything else save a person? No. Just faith alone in Christ alone.

Do you give God, pay God, perform for God in any way at all? No. Just faith alone in Christ alone.

To believe in Jesus includes *unbelieving* in everything else.

When I was a youth pastor, I had a Bible study near the biggest high school in Illinois — every week, students crowded in. All I did was open the Bible and speak.

Dozens of students got saved. One of them was captain of the football team. His name was Ed, and he went on to go to Bible school and to serve as a missionary.

On Ed's very first week at Bible study, he told me that I said something that pinned him to his seat.

I quoted John 3:16:

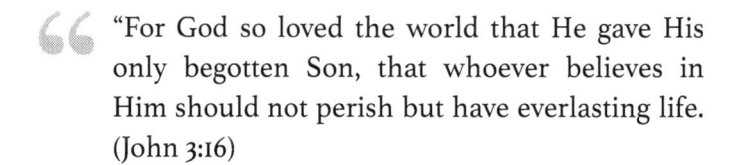

> "For God so loved the world that He gave His only begotten Son, that whoever believes in Him should not perish but have everlasting life. (John 3:16)

But when I quoted it, I filled in the word "believes in him" with different words:

Whoever is baptized? Whoever is a good person? Whoever goes to church? Whoever is religious enough?

And on and on.

Until I finally brought it home. Whoever believes in Him.

Ed said that he felt pinned to his seat by those words.

All throughout the Gospel is this concept called grace. Grace is the wonderful truth that God does all the work to save us. God Himself bears the burden for you to be forgiven, justified, and given eternal life.

No explanation of the Gospel is correct that leaves the burden on your shoulders. The burden is God's.

Whatever language you use, that's the key.

Here are some verses to use, and to write down in the front of your Bible.

- For God so loved the world that He gave His only begotten Son, that whoever believes in Him should not perish but have everlasting life. (John 3:16)
- Therefore, having been justified by faith, we have peace with God through our Lord Jesus Christ, (Romans 5:1)
- For by grace you have been saved through faith, and that not of yourselves; it is the gift of God, not of works, lest anyone should boast. (Ephesians 2:8, 9)

CHOOSE

When a person admits their sinfulness, and when a person states they believe in Jesus, they are mainly doing something in their *minds* — they are acknowledging certain things to be true.

But faith also includes an act of the *will*. This act of the will is supported and enabled by the divine power of the Holy Spirit as the Gospel is being communicated.

CHOOSE... Tell God right now that you are choosing to receive Jesus as your Savior and only hope.

A person can choose, no matter how they feel.

A person can choose, no matter how many doubts they have.

A person can choose, no matter how weak.

A person can choose, no matter how ready or not ready.

A person can choose, no matter how sinful.

> And whosoever will, let him take the water of life freely. (Revelation 22:17b, KJV)

They have admitted their need.
They have confessed that they believe in Jesus.
All that's left is to make it official. Make the choice. State the choice. Believe the Gospel.

Here are some verses you might use (and write down in the front of your Bible):

- Come to Me, all you who labor and are heavy laden, and I will give you rest. (Matthew 11:28)
- Whoever desires, let him take the water of life freely. (Revelation 22:17b)
- But as many as received Him, to them He gave the right to become children of God, to those who believe in His name: (John 1:12)

THE PRAYER

The time for talk is over. Now, it's time to actually tie the knot!

The simplest way I've found to do that is to lead your friend through an ABC prayer. You can tell them one line at a time, and ask them to repeat it to God.

Here's a sample prayer.

ADMIT: God I admit I'm a sinner. I've disobeyed You. I admit that I can never solve my sin problem on my own. I need You.

BELIEVE: God, I believe that Jesus died on the Cross for me and rose again. I believe He died for my sins and rose again. My sins are paid in full by Jesus Christ. God, I believe that no amount of religion, good works, or living clean could ever pay for my sins — just Jesus. I don't get how it all works, but right now, I'm believing in Jesus.

CHOOSE: God, right now I choose to trust in Jesus as my only hope. I choose Him as my Savior. I receive Him. And, I'm asking You as best as I can, right now, please save me, please forgive me, and please make me Your child forever. Thank You, God, in Jesus' name, Amen.

THEN WHAT?

What an incredible moment! Do you realize you have just witnessed God's greatest miracle? New birth! New life! The transition from the domain of darkness into the kingdom of God's beloved Son!

Sitting before you is a royal child of our Great King. What can be better than that?

What should you do? Give them a cheer or even a hug, and say, *"Welcome's to God's Family!"*

Which brings up the fact that this new believer is also a spiritual child.

Just as you wouldn't leave a physical child to fend for themselves, you wouldn't want to leave a spiritual child to fend for themselves.

So now what do you do?

1. Welcome them into God's Family.
2. Say a simple, easily understood prayer for them. Pray for assurance and confidence based on the promises of God's Word.
3. Give them a copy of *Welcome to God's Family,* the

first book in this series. It's good to always keep a few in stock.

That's enough for now. You don't want to overwhelm a new believer in Jesus. It's a strange new world for them. Be kind.

Over the coming weeks and months, you will want to help them get involved in a good church.

Even more importantly, you will to lovingly lead them through the Grace Pathway. That way, they will learn their new labels and their new privileges as a child of the joyful, radiant, fully-blessed family of God.

You have led a person to Christ. What a privilege! What an honor! Grace has flowed through you and a new life is born.

Well done.

May God increase your tribe. Can you imagine thousands of ambassadors for Jesus, ready and equipped to share the Gospel, all spread out throughout our town? In every business. In every subdivision. In every store and classroom and government office!

It is my prayer that God will continue to use you in amazing ways to help your friends find and follow God—as you both *live* and *share* your faith.

WHAT'S NEXT?

God is eager for you to know Him more and more. I'm praying for you! Keep Growing along the Grace Pathway.

Milestone 4 is called "God Uses You."

4.1 — Living and Sharing Your Faith (this book)
4.2 — Discover Your Gifts
4.3 — Know Why You Believe (Apologetics)

You've come so far. Keep going and keep growing so you can know all the treasures that are yours because you belong to God.

You'll find these books and more resources at: www.maxgrace.com

---

VERITAS SCHOOL OF BIBLICAL MINISTRY

You're ready now to take your biblical instruction to seminary level teaching.

We have created a seminary for people who never thought it would be possible.

How will you feel a year from now when your friend asks a question, and your answer displays a wisdom that surprises even yourself?

Earn your Master of Ministry Certification and take your service for Christ and the Gospel deeper and higher than you ever thought possible.

Find out more at www.VeritasSchool.life

Made in the USA
Columbia, SC
09 January 2022